NEVER MIND THE CANARIES

D1337823

NEVER MIND THE CANARIES

The Ultimate NORWICH CITY QUIZ BOOK

EDWARD COUZENS-LAKE

The History Press

This book is dedicated to all Norwich City supporters.
On the Ball, City!

First published 2015

Reprinted 2015

The History Press
The Mill, Brimscombe Port
Stroud, Gloucestershire, GL5 2QG
www.thehistorypress.co.uk

© Edward Couzens-Lake, 2015

The right of Edward Couzens-Lake to be identified as the
Author of this work has been asserted in accordance with the
Copyright, Designs and Patents Act 1988.

British Library Cataloguing in Publication Data.
A catalogue record for this book is available from the British Library.

ISBN 978 0 7509 6207 0

Typesetting and origination by The History Press
Printed and bound in Great Britain

Contents

Rob Butler, ex-Canary legend Grant Holt, and Paul McVeigh
compete in a spot of 'Canary Mastermind' on BBC Radio Norfolk.

Foreword by Rob Butler

I'd known Ed for a while through other books that he'd written, or else when he'd appeared on shows at Radio Norfolk to talk about the game and projects he was involved with, and soon realised he'd be the ideal person to set the questions for the regular feature that Macca (Paul) and I wanted to include in 'McVeigh & Butler' which we called 'Canary Mastermind'.

It was a bit of fun, a chance for our studio guests to show off their knowledge of the Canaries by answering a few questions about the club. For some of the players who came on as guests we made it a bit easier by getting Ed to set questions about themselves and their own careers, confident that they'd get most of them right, accepting the fact that their overall knowledge of the club might not have been as comprehensive as that of the fans!

Amongst the players who came along and had a go were Grant Holt, Darren Huckerby, John Ruddy, Darren Eadie, Jeremy Goss, Leon McKenzie, Tony Spearing, Neil Adams and Gary Holt.

Gossy came on the show with Ed, who hadn't told him beforehand that he was doing a quiz about himself live on air, so it was a bit of a surprise for him – especially as Gossy doesn't like quizzes! – but he got most of them right nonetheless.

Grant Holt disputed just about every answer Ed gave to his questions about him whilst Hucks thought he'd scored loads more goals than Ed had listed. Neil Adams and Gary Holt did it together and showed as good a knowledge about each other's careers as they did their own.

Some players were ever so competitive about it, like Elliott Bennett who treated it all very seriously and got nearly all of them right, as did Darren Eadie and a few others who gave additional, previously unknown details to some of the answers they gave. That, for me, is one of the great things about Canary Mastermind, the fact that someone can answer a question and then go on to tell a little story relating to it, which is always really interesting to hear.

It's something that was, and remains, a bit of a light-hearted interlude on the shows. But people do take it seriously, sometimes arguing with the answer given and, more often than not, wanting to know how many points a teammate or friend got so they can do whatever's needed to beat them in order to get the banter in!

This book will give all Canaries the chance to test each other on their Norwich City FC knowledge. And I bet everyone will be just as committed to getting one up on their mates by getting more right than them, else quoting that certain little detail from the club's history that no one else will know.

I expect I'll have a copy about me somewhere on some of the longer away trips. Except I'm going to be the question master this time – it'll be easier than having to try to know the answer to some obscure fact about a game played in 1969. Because, knowing Ed, there'll be a few in here like that.

Enjoy.

OTBC!

Rob Butler
BBC Radio Norfolk presenter and Canary fan

Foreword by Paul McVeigh

Norwich City fans know their football.

I know this because I've talked to them on the radio phone-ins that I've done on BBC Radio Norfolk with Rob and you can be sure that if you're making a comment about a previous game or a player from the past, whenever it was, they'll come right back at you with all the relevant information needed.

Past players, matches, games won, lost or drawn, goals scored and points won or lost. It's like talking to an encyclopaedia sometimes!

When we did Canary Mastermind in the studio, I'd be sat there without a clue, sometimes I didn't even have the beginnings of an answer in my head, and I'd say 'Oh come *on*, how on earth is anyone meant to remember THAT?'

Yet Ed, who set the questions, clearly knew that most Norwich fans would as, more often than not, they got the answer right.

Ask away, ask them anything.

Scorer of the Norwich goal in the 1–0 win over Aston Villa in October 1982? No problem. Opponents in first game to be played at Carrow Road? Easy. Player signed for £50,000 from Bournemouth in 1977? Got that, next?

As someone who had a go at the quiz himself one week and didn't do so well, I was always hugely impressed with the people who'd come on and get most of them right without hesitation or the need for a clue.

It says a lot about Norwich fans' love and respect for their team. Their interest and devotion to the Canaries is not just about the now, it's about the club as a whole – including the rich legacy of its history; players, managers and matches included.

So it's good to see that Ed and The History Press have got together to do a quiz book all about the club, so everyone can have a go at showing off their knowledge about the Canaries; a book that will, I'm sure, come out on some of the longer away trips (that would be all of them then) and maybe start a few arguments into the bargain.

I loved my time playing for Norwich City; one of the reasons for that was the club's fans. They always provided great support, home or away, there in numbers and always loud and colourful. It was great to play in front of them and to celebrate with them whenever I scored a goal. Now, how many would that be and in how many appearances I wonder?

Enjoy it!

Paul McVeigh
Broadcaster and former Canary

Acknowledgements

First and foremost to The History Press. To Matilda Richards for commissioning me to write this book and Ruth Boyes for editing it. Thank you.

Rob Butler and Paul McVeigh for their contributions and for entrusting Canary Mastermind to me on their show on BBC Radio Norfolk. I know Holty said some of my answers to his questions were wrong. They weren't.

To Chris Goreham. 'CHANNNNNCEE!'

Peter Rogers and all at Norwich City FC. The support and backing you and the club always lend me in my various projects is, and will always be, hugely appreciated.

Chris Rushby and all at Jarrold Books in Norwich.

Likewise to all at Waterstones in Norwich.

And to my wife Sarah for her tolerance and patience with me in absolutely everything!

How This
Book Works

Football trivia, questions and minutiae.
They're what make the world go round. Honestly,
they do. Just ask Albert Einstein. That famous equation,
you know the one, $E=mc^2$?

The E stands for football trivia, a little-known but crucial
fact. Einstein knew the score. In fact, as a scientific genius and
visionary, he often applied his massive intelligence to football
tactics, advocating the now widespread 4-2-3-1 system long
before anyone else did. Football's loss was, unquestionably,
science's gain. Just think what he could have done on the
blackboard in the home team dressing room; never mind
all those complicated formulas and calculations, he'd have
devised and chalked up a way to defeat Arsenal's offside trap
in no time.

He would have known what item is brought to the
FA Cup Final every year but never used – as, of course, will
you, dear reader, knowing such things is part of the very
foundation of footballing trivia so I'm not going to give the
answer here. No, far from it. You're here because you moved
away from the basics and on to a specialist subject, namely
anything and everything to do with our great club and our
shared passion … Norwich City FC.

The boys in yellow and green. Except they weren't always.
The Canaries. Except they weren't always that either.

Carrow Road. Well, for at least part of our history anyway. This book is for you.

And, first and very much foremost, it's a quiz book.

So it contains no recipes, no funny pictures of cats or any celebrity gossip of any kind. If that's what you are after, then put this book down and walk slowly away. There's nothing for you to see here.

I'm asking the questions, you're providing the answers. And every question is about Norwich City Football Club. You'll find no Manchester United or Liverpool in here, no Chelsea either. So, again, if they are your thing then move along quietly please. Thank you.

Obviously the book aims to be as up to date as possible. The questions will, therefore, cover the history of the club, right from its early days through to the latter part of the 2014/15 Championship season. Obviously, as time goes on, some of the answers to the questions might change – records are there to be broken, as are facts, figures and statistics. All of the answers are therefore believed to be correct as of March 2015.

So bear that in mind if, for example, we changed our name to the Norwich City Yellow Terrors after that date or moved to a purpose-built 60,000-capacity stadium on Eaton Golf Course, then that'll be why there is no mention of them in the book. That and anything else that happened after my deadline door (Jim White voice) 'slammed shut', because, as far as I'm concerned, it hasn't happened yet.

I've researched and devised every one of the thirty rounds of questions and answers myself. Where I haven't been absolutely sure of something I've checked, and double-checked, with an independent source – the club, another book or publication or a fellow fan and Canary devotee.

But, ultimately, all of the information written down in this book is my responsibility and mine alone – so if anything is wrong then it's down to me and I freely admit to the error. But hopefully there won't be any mistakes.

Whether it is for whiling away the miles spent on a coach, train or in the car to or from an away game; a boring afternoon in the office; or to settle an on-going classroom or office debate – or, indeed, to start one – if it's Norwich City related, then you have all the questions, as well as all the answers (apart from that one about what goes to the FA Cup Final every year but is never used), right here, in this book.

Some will be easy. Some will be hard. Some of them may make you realise that there are some things you didn't already know. Others will be a bit tenuous, even silly, some straightforward and others annoying. But they will all, one way or the other, have a connection, somehow, somewhere along the line, to the Canaries. A player, a game, a goal, a manager, an incident … something.

So get your yellow and green tinted glasses on and start asking them. Let's see who knows what.

I hope you enjoy the book and the debate and disagreement it might create. Which is, I guess, the whole point.

OTBC!

Edward Couzens-Lake

Round

1

In the Beginning

So, welcome to the main part of the book. The preliminaries are out of the way and we're into the nitty-gritty. And there is no place better to start, surely, than right at the beginning, the dawn of Norwich City. This round deals with the formation of, and very early years of, the club – opening with a nice easy one to get you started.

1 In what year was Norwich City formed?

2 Where was the meeting that led to the club's formation held?

3 What high street retailer now occupies that building?

4 Where was the club's first ground?

5 Which league were the club elected to after their formation?

6 Which team were the opposition for Norwich City's first-ever match?

7   What colour were the club's first shirts?

8   What is the first line of 'On the Ball, City'?

9   What was the club's nickname when it was formed?

10 Who was the club's first manager?

11 Which First Division side did Norwich City, then in the Southern League, knock out of the 1914/15 FA Cup?

Round
2

Into the Big Time!

Taking a look at the 1971/72 season – hugely significant in terms of the club's history as it saw us promoted to the top flight of English football for the very first time as Division Two Champions.

1   Which three players appeared in every one of the club's 42 league games that season?

2   Who ended that season as our top scorer in the league with 13 goals?

3   The biggest league attendance at Carrow Road that season was an eye-watering 34,914. Who were the opponents?

4   Who made his Canary debut, wearing the number 9 shirt, in the 1–1 draw at Sunderland on 9 October 1971?

5   Which club did Norwich sign Jimmy Bone from in February 1972?

6 'We feel this young man has all the capabilities required and that with any luck at all he can be a great asset to this club' – who said this about promotion-winning Norwich manager, Ron Saunders?

7 Which team beat Norwich 4–0 on 4 March 1972?

8 The Canaries made it to the quarter-finals of the League Cup during this season. Which team knocked us out at that stage?

9 Dave Stringer's header in the 1–1 draw at Watford on 29 April 1972 sealed the Second Division title for Norwich, but who scored the Watford goal on that day?

10 Norwich went up that season as Division Two Champions, who were league runners-up?

11 Which Norwich player came on as a substitute on 12 separate occasions in league games that season, contributing a total of 3 goals from the bench?

Round
3

Canaries
Before and After

This round looks at the achievements, or otherwise, of Norwich players in their playing days, before they joined the club or after they had left. Each of the eleven questions names a footballing fact or incident, all you have to do is name the player involved. Remember, he would either have previously been a Norwich player or have gone on to join us at a later date.

For example – scored 2 goals for West Ham in the 1975 FA Cup Final. Answer – Alan Taylor.*

1   Kept a clean sheet at Wembley in the 1978 League Cup Final.

2   Became known as 'Supersub' at his previous English club.

3   Scored 4 goals against Manchester United at Old Trafford in August 1969.

4   Captained the side that beat Norwich in the 1973
    League Cup Final.

5   Scored the goal that confirmed Norwich's qualification
    for the 1993/94 UEFA Cup.

6   Plays the role of Sammy Davis Junior in *The Rat Pack*
    musical tribute show.

7   Played for Scotland in their 3–2 win over Holland in the
    1978 World Cup Finals.

8   Was an unused substitute in the 1984 European Cup Final.

9   Won the Man of the Match Award in the 1995
    FA Cup Final.

10 Scored 9 goals in an FA Cup game.

11 Played for Arsenal against Ipswich Town in the 1978
    FA Cup Final.

*Alan Taylor ended up having two playing spells at Norwich.
He originally joined us from the Hammers in August 1979
before signing for the club a second time after he'd left Bury,
in August 1988.

Consolation Goals

We've all been there to witness the boys in yellow and green get a good hiding at the hands of the opposition. Listed below are eleven such examples. Can you name the Norwich goalscorer in these games, the man who at least gave us a little something to cheer on the day?

1   Norwich City 1–7 Colchester United (August 2009).

2   Rotherham 4–1 Norwich City (August 1981).

3   Blackburn 7–1 Norwich City (October 1992).

4   Sheffield Wednesday 4–1 Norwich City (May 2008).

5   Middlesbrough 6–1 Norwich City (October 1980).

6   Torquay United 7–1 Norwich City (February 1957).

7   Norwich City 1–4 Derby County (April 1969).

8   Norwich City 1–5 Manchester City (December 2011).

9   Crystal Palace 5–1 Norwich City (October 1998).

10   Port Vale 6–1 Norwich City (December 1996).

11   Newcastle 5–1 Norwich City (March 1977).

Round

5

Loan Canaries

From short-term signings of the sublime to the borrowing of the ridiculous, the Canaries have made full use of the loan system over the years. The eleven questions below relate to such deals.

1　Signed from Crystal Palace in February 1972 and, in doing so, became the Canaries first-ever loan player.

2　One of four goalkeepers used in Norwich's 46 league games in the 2009/10 season, he came in from Tottenham Hotspur and played in 3 league games.

3　League Championship and FA Cup-winning international midfielder, signed in 1995, who made a total of 5 appearances during his time with us, scoring 1 goal.

4　Norwich City signed fifteen different players on loan during the 2008/09 season – how many of them can you name?

5 Darren Huckerby and Peter Crouch were two of three Premier League players signed on loan for the Canaries by Nigel Worthington in September 2003. Who was the other member of the trio?

6 Awarded the FA Cup winner's medal in 1970, signed on loan for the Canaries in 1976, playing in 3 league games.

7 Signed on loan from Sheffield Wednesday in October 1983 but limited to 1 appearance for the club, a 16-minute cameo as a late substitute in the 3–3 draw against Manchester United in October 1983.

8 Former Tottenham manager who had a loan spell with Norwich City during the 1974/75 season.

9 Joined Norwich on loan in 2008 and has since won a Champions League winner's medal.

10 Signed from Swindon Town before being immediately loaned back to that club in September 2014.

11 Former England midfielder who joined Norwich on loan from Charlton Athletic in October 2000.

Round

6

The League Cup

For this round we're going to take a look at the club's history in the League Cup in all its guises, a tournament that, on the whole, we haven't done too badly in.

1 Who was Norwich City's manager when the club won the League Cup for the first time in 1962?

2 On what ground was the first leg of that year's final played?

3 Norwich beat Ipswich 4–2 at Portman Road in the competition's second round in September 1968, name the future Scottish international striker who scored a hat-trick for Norwich on that day?

4 Name the Sunderland player who scored the own goal that won Norwich the 1985 League Cup Final at Wembley.

5 One of the players in Sunderland's losing side in 1985 later went on to join the Canaries, who was it?

6   Norwich won their first-ever game in the League Cup 6–2 in October 1960, who were our luckless opponents?

7   Who conceded the handball that resulted in the penalty that won the 1975 League Cup Final for Aston Villa against Norwich?

8   Norwich reached the semi-finals of the League Cup in 1974 only to be denied at the last hurdle by which club?

9   Two of the victorious Tottenham team members, from their 1973 League Cup Final success against Norwich, later on went to play for Norwich, name them.

10   In what year did the Jarvis brothers, Rossi and Ryan, line up for the Canaries in the same team for the first time in a League Cup tie against Rotherham United?

11   Which two Norwich players scored their first goals for the club in the 2–3 win at Watford in the League Cup third round in September 2013?

Round 7

Who Was the First?

There's a first time for everything and that's what this round is about. There are plenty of milestones in football and what we are looking for here is the name of the Norwich City player who was the first to achieve it for the Canaries.

Who, therefore, was the first Norwich player or manager …

1 To score a goal for the Canaries in the Premier League?

2 To lift a trophy at Wembley?

3 To spend at least £1 million on a player?

4 To play for England?

5 To come on as a substitute?

6 To score a hat-trick in the old First Division (pre-Premier League)?

7 To play at the 'new' Wembley Stadium?

8   To score an own goal in the Premier League?

9   To both play for and manage the club?

10   To be red-carded in the Premier League?

11   To score in a competitive European game?

From Which Club?

A simple, straightforward, no fuss or bother round this.
Listed below are the names of eleven Norwich City players,
all you have to do is name the club we signed them from.

1   Tim Sherwood.

2   Ted MacDougall.

3   David Phillips.

4   John Ryan.

5   Chris Woods.

6   Joe Royle.

7   Steve Bruce.

8   Conor McGrandles.

9   Mike Channon.

10   Elliott Bennett.

11   Mike Phelan.

Round 9

The 1970s:
Part 1

Ah yes, the footballing decade of tight perms and even tighter shorts. Plus *Match of the Week* and the dulcet tones of Gerry Harrison on a Sunday afternoon helping celebrate what was a rather busy decade for the boys in yellow and green. Fingers on buzzers, no conferring, here we go …

1   Who was the manager of Norwich City on 1 January 1970?

2   Who was the club's top goalscorer (league and cup) for the 1970/71 season?

3   Name the three Canaries who played in all 42 of the club's league games during their title-winning Division Two 1971/72 season?

4   Norwich lost 4–0 in their league game at Birmingham City on 4 March 1972, who made his Canary debut in that game?

CANARIES

NORWICH CITY F.C.
v MANCHESTER UNITED

Saturday, 28th September 1974.　Kick-off 3 p.m.

SECOND DIVISION　Official Programme
Volume 3 Number 6　**10p**

5   Birmingham eventually finished that season as runners-up
    with us Champions. Which team finished in third place?

6   Just I appearance for this Norwich City striker in the
    1971/72 season – as a substitute in the 0–1 defeat
    against Chelsea in the League Cup fifth round on
    17 November – can you name him?

7   Which team did Norwich City register their first-ever
    top-flight league victory over?

8   The Canaries reached the 1973 League Cup Final at
    Wembley, scoring 15 goals in the 6 games it took us
    to get there, who was the club's top scorer in the
    competition that season?

9   Name the cup competition (in addition to the FA and
    League cups) that the Canaries entered from 1973
    to 1975?

10 Which team beat Norwich 3–1 at Carrow Road on 17 November 1973, precipitating the resignation of Ron Saunders immediately after that match?

11 Norwich reached the semi-finals of the 1974 League Cup only to lose over two legs to which team?

Football's Gone Too Commercial

Has it? A moot point I suppose. Yes, kick-off times are mucked around with and sponsors' names are creeping more and more into the game. But where would the game be without all of their money? These questions relate to that side of the game and how it has touched, one way or another, our beloved Canaries.

1 Who were our shirt sponsors when we won the 1985 League Cup?

2 And by what horrendous corporate name was the competition known as that season?

3 A kit manufacturer's logo first appeared on a Norwich City shirt in the 1975/76 season – whose logo was it?

4 From 1989–92 the shirt promoted a certain company's 'sports shoes' – which company was it?

5   What was unusual about the home kit from 1997 to 1999?

6   Our 3–1 win over Nottingham Forest on 31 August 1992 was shown live on Sky Sports. Who sponsored the show (i.e.) 'Sky Sports and *x* proudly present *x* Monday Night Football'?

7   Which company sponsored the Division One game at Carrow Road against Liverpool on 20 March 1976, the first example of outside sponsorship at Carrow Road?

8   Name the cup tournament that the Canaries were invited to play in during the 1985/86 season as 'compensation' for not being able to play in that season's UEFA Cup following the ban on all English clubs in Europe post-Heysel?

9   Aviva first sponsored the club's shirts in 2008; which company manufactured the kit for that 2008/09 season?

10 Name the company who manufactured the Norwich City kit from 1999 to 2001?

11 Which company sponsored the club's kit before Aviva took over in 2008?

Round

II

Norwich are on the Telly Again

Lock the front door, close the curtains. Norwich are on the telly. The following eleven questions all related to games featuring the Canaries that were broadcast live on either the BBC, ITV or Sky. Can you hear us on the box?

1 Who scored Norwich's second goal in the 2–1 win at Carrow Road over West Ham on 17 December 1988, our first-ever 'live' appearance in a league game? (ITV)

2 Manchester United inflicted near-terminal damage on the Canaries' 1992/93 Premier League title hopes with their 3–1 win at Carrow Road on 5 April 1993. Who scored the Norwich goal in that match? (Sky)

3 Who was the Canaries' substitute (only one back then!) in their 1985 League Cup Final line-up against Sunderland? (BBC)

4 Name the last Norwich player to touch the ball before
   Jeremy Goss famously volleyed the opening goal in the
   Canaries 2–1 win over Bayern Munich in the UEFA Cup
   second-round match on 19 October 1993? (Sky)

5 Name all three scorers in the Canaries 3–1 win over
   Nottingham Forest on 31 August 1992, our first fixture
   to be televised live by Sky? (Sky)

6 Why was our 2–0 win at Carrow Road over Stockport on
   21 April 2002 significant, result-wise? (ITV)

7 'It could get worse for Ipswich. It *has* got worse for
   Ipswich!' – who has just scored for Norwich against
   you-know-who in 2010? (BBC)

8 Who was Brian Moore's co-commentator during our 3–2
   win against Millwall at The Den on 22 January 1989? (ITV)

9 Who scored Norwich's decisive goal in the 1–0 win over
   Tottenham at Carrow Road on 23 February 2014? (Sky)

10 Who was the match commentator for our 2001/02
Division One play-off final game against Birmingham at
the Millennium Stadium? (ITV)

11 Who were our opposition in the televised game in
April 2010 that saw Paul Lambert banished from the
dugout by referee Eddie Ilderton? (Sky)

Ever-present

Here are eleven ever-presents for you to identify, all players who have appeared in every one of the Canaries' league matches throughout at least one complete season – which may, or may not, be mentioned.

1 Goalkeeper signed from QPR, an ever-present in four out of the six seasons he spent at Carrow Road.

2 League ever-present and the club's leading scorer in the 1977/78 season.

3 Appeared 662 times for the Canaries in total, a genuine club legend.

4 Great Yarmouth-born and leader of men on and off the pitch.

5 Awarded an FA Cup winner's medal with Arsenal in 1979.

6 A Canary great whose name adorns a trophy.

7   Canary captain in the 1988/89 season.

8   Norwich City's all-time leading league goalscorer.

9   Midfielder, one of three league ever-presents during our first Premier League season.

10 Scottish striker who Lol Morgan maybe sold a little prematurely.

11 Striker cum full-back who went on to win the FA Cup with Coventry City.

Round

13

Record Breakers

Eleven questions dedicated to Canary records – old, new, obscure and broken. Will the 2015/16 season see any of them surpassed?

1　The club's record win was 10–2 in a Division Three South fixture back in 1930. Who were the hapless, not to say hopeless, opposition?

2　What was the score and who were our opponents in our record victory in the FA Cup?

3　In which season did Norwich go a club-record 25 consecutive league games without a win?

4　Which player was Norwich's first £1 million signing in 1994?

5　Who holds the record for most international appearances for his country whilst at Norwich City?

6   The man who has scored the most league goals in one season for the Canaries did so with 31 goals from 45 appearances, name him?

7   Who was the first Norwich City player to make an appearance for his country in the finals of a World Cup whilst he was at the club?

8   What are our highest- and lowest-ever league finishes (positions and table at the end of a competitive league season)?

9   Which Norwich City manager holds the club record for the most games whilst he was in charge of the club?

10 Ron Ashman broke the then Norwich City transfer record with the purchase of a Luton Town centre forward for £35,000 in September 1963, name the player?

11 Who scored the club's first-ever goals in the First Division, the Premier League, the UEFA Cup and the twenty-first century?

Britain's Number One

The eleven songs listed below were all, at some point, No. 1 in the UK Top 40. Your task is to connect the song to whoever or whatever was happening at Norwich City whilst it was top of the proverbial pops.

For example, Phillip Bailey and Phil Collins – 'Easy Lover' (game), would be the 1985 Milk Cup Final win over Sunderland.

In the case of it being at the top of the charts on more than one occasion, please answer for when it first appeared there.

If you're finding this one really, REALLY hard, the years in question are listed at the end of the round.

1 Queen – 'Bohemian Rhapsody'
   (Norwich City manager?)

2 Nilsson – 'Without You'
   (Recalled Norwich City captain?)

3   Chuck Berry – 'My Ding-a-Ling'
    (Norwich City player's famous cup hat-trick?)

4   Fun featuring Janelle Monae – 'We Are Young'
    (Canary hero departs?)

5   The Specials – 'The Specials AKA Live EP'
    ('Oooh, what a goal, that's a magnificent goal'?)

6   Ozzy and Kelly Osbourne – 'Changes'
    (Hucks says farewell – or does he?)

7   Freddie Mercury – 'Living On My Own'
    (Fox cross and Gossy volley?)

8   Rick Astley – 'Never Gonna Give You Up'
    (Norwich City shirt sponsor?)

9   Black Eyed Peas – 'I Gotta Feeling'
    (Canary keeper's nightmare debut?)

10 Conway Twitty – 'It's Only Make Believe'
    ('Bly Bly Babes'?)

11 Art Garfunkel – 'Bright Eyes'
    (Norwich City leading goalscorer at the end of the season?)

Hint. (The years in question):

1 – 1975; 2 – 1972; 3 – 1972; 4 – 2012;
5 – 1979; 6 – 2003; 7 – 1993; 8 – 1987;
9 – 2008; 10 – 1959; 11 – 1979.

Round

15

The 1980s:
Part 1

Perms, ponytails and mullets. It was all about the haircuts.
And leg warmers. Plus Saint & Greavsie on ITV. Not that they
featured us much. Unless they had to. It's the Quiz of the
Decade and it's about Norwich City. Concentrate now …

1 The Canaries won their opening game of the 1980/81
   season against Stoke City 5–1. Name the Canary
   goalscorers? (A special smartarse mark if you can name
   the Stoke City scorer as well.)

2 Name the three players whose surname began with a
   W who Ken Brown signed for Norwich during the
   1980/81 season?

3 The Canaries were promoted at the end of the 1981/82
   season. Which two clubs were promoted to Division
   One alongside us?

4   Who was the club's leading goalscorer that
    (1981/82) season?

5   In their first game of the 1982/83 season the Canaries
    lost 2–1 to Manchester City, managed by John Bond, at
    Carrow Road. A former Norwich City player opened
    the scoring for Bond's side, who was it?

6   Name the Norwich City player called up by England for
    the first time at the end of the 1982/83 season for an
    international trip to Australia?

7   Name the ex-Tottenham and Arsenal defender who
    made his Canary debut on the opening day of the
    1983/84 season?

8   The Canaries were 3–0 down to Manchester United
    at Carrow Road after an hour of the league clash on
    1 October 1983, yet came back to draw the game 3–3.
    Who were the Norwich goalscorers?

9   Two strikers whose surname began with the letter C
    made at least one senior league appearance for the
    Canaries during the 1983/84 season, one was Mike
    Channon – who was the other?

10 Two goalkeepers who have played for England at full
    international level played for Norwich in the 1984/85
    season, can you name them?

11 Whose handball gave Sunderland their penalty against
    us in the 1985 League Cup Final?

Round 16

Great Scots

The Canaries have been truly blessed with many fine footballers whose origins have come from north of the border. The following questions are about some of the great and good men of Scotland who have graced the turf at Carrow Road and the City of Norwich.

1 Signed for the Canaries in 1984, former clubs included Nottingham Forest and Everton.

2 Scored 66 goals in 138 league games for Norwich, a former Hammer turned Canary.

3 Joined us for a then club-record fee of £580,000.

4 Won a UEFA Cup Winners Cup Medal* prior to joining Norwich.

5 An ever-present in the 1959 FA Cup side, signed from Partick Thistle for just £500.

6   Part of the Motherwell side that finished as Scottish Premier League runners-up to Rangers in 1995.

7   Once of Celtic, played for and managed the Canaries.

8   'On the wing' with this goalscoring promotion winner of 1972.

9   A man of whom *The Times* once said, '… got his customary booking; the referee ought to take his name in the changing room rather than on the pitch thus saving time'.

10 Two-time Player of the Year at Rugby Park before joining the Canaries.

11 There were 256 league appearances for this son of Lothian, who later gave much of his time to non-league Yarmouth Town and Diss Town as their manager.

*Also known as the European Cup Winners Cup.

The 1970s:
Part 2

Remember *Football Focus* with Bob Wilson? Bob started hosting the BBC's lunchtime football preview show in 1974, inheriting the slot from Sam Leitch who hosted its predecessor, the imaginatively titled *Football Preview*, until Bob's arrival on the scene. Sam is perhaps best known (or not, as the case may be) for the famous line he uttered when, after a big victory for Scottish side Raith Rovers, he said, 'They'll be dancing in the streets of Raith tonight', a remark which has long been attributed to the late David Coleman, amongst others. Whether or not Sam ever had cause to wonder if there was, or might have been, dancing on the streets of Norwich for any reason is open to conjecture …

I   Name the former Ipswich Town midfielder who made his Norwich City debut in the opening league game of the 1974/75 season?

2 Which side did the Canaries beat over two legs in the 1975 League Cup Semi-Final?

3 Which Fourth Division side knocked Norwich out of the 1976 FA Cup?

4 John Bond signed another ex-Bournemouth player when he signed centre half David Jones early on in the 1975/76 season – but which club did Jones leave in order to join Norwich?

5 Ted MacDougall left Norwich for Southampton in September 1976, who did the Canaries immediately buy to replace him?

6 An FA Cup winner from 1970 joined the Canaries on loan during the 1976/77 season, name him?

7 Graham Souness scored against Norwich in the Canaries' opening home game of the 1977/78 campaign, who was Souness playing for at the time?

8 What did the Canaries fail to do in 23 consecutive matches during the 1977/78 season?

9   Norwich entered two minor cup competitions during the 1978/79 season, name them?

10 Which US club did Norwich sign former Aberdeen striker Davie Robb from in September 1978?

11 The Canaries signed two members of West Ham's 1975 FA Cup-winning side in the summer of 1979, who were they?

Round

18

Obscure is the Word: Part 1

A round for the real trivia kings and queens, one that reminds us that life and the Canaries isn't all Premier League glory, Bayern Munich, Wembley wins and feeling the love for a Peters, MacDougall, Huckerby or Holt. This is the round that Norwich City history might otherwise have forgotten, hard-core yellow and green minutiae to challenge the very best out there. Let us play …

1 The Canaries signed five players on loan during our League One title-winning season of 2009/10, name them?

2 The club has not always been known as the Canaries – what was the club's original nickname?

3 Norwich finished in twentieth place in the old Division One in the 1972/73 season – what was special about their finishing in that position at the end of that particular campaign?

4 Who was the first player to score against Norwich in the Premier League?

5 Jeremy Goss scored his famous Goal of the Month volley against Leeds United in the 4–0 win on 21 August 1993, who scored the other Norwich goals on that day?

6   The Canaries famously reached the FA Cup Semi-Finals as
    a Third Division club, beating such footballing luminaries
    as Manchester United and Tottenham en route, but
    who did we beat in the competition's first round
    that season?

7   Who was the player Norwich City sold in order to,
    as he later quipped, '... pay for the undersoil heating'?

8   Which Norwich City manager signed former Wales
    striker John Hartson on loan from West Bromwich
    Albion in 2007?

9   Name the Norwich City player who moved to Blackpool
    in 2008 as part of the deal that saw Wes Hoolahan join
    the Canaries?

10 Which player said, when asked what he knew about the
    Canaries when he joined them in 1957, '... only that they
    are bankrupt'.

11 The Canaries scored 17 goals in their run to the FA Cup
    semi-finals in 1989, who was the club's top scorer in the
    competition that season?

The FA Cup

OK, so we've never won the FA Cup. Not yet anyway – but there's always next season. We've had some good runs and some great results in the competition though and these questions all relate to Norwich City and '… the greatest knock-out cup competition in the world' – according to whoever happens to be televising the live games that particular season. To those that aren't, funnily enough, it's an out-dated irrelevance competed for by teams playing their shadow sides and hardly worth mentioning!

1 We've reached the FA Cup semi-finals on three occasions but in which years?

2 Brighton & Hove Albion beat us in the 1983 quarter-finals, who was Norwich City's captain on that day?

3 It took us 4 games and 7 hours of football to do what in the 1984/85 competition?

4 Luton Town could be considered to be our FA Cup nemesis, opponents-wise, taking into consideration what happened in the 1927, 1959 and 2013 competitions – what happened to us in each of those years?

5 What did we achieve in the FA Cup for seven consecutive seasons from 1969 to 1975?

6 How many times did Norwich get to at least the quarter-finals of the FA Cup during the 1990s?

7 Who was the Norwich goalkeeper in our 1–0 win over Tottenham in the competition's fifth-round replay in February 1959?

8 Name the Glasgow-born central defender who made his one and only senior start for Norwich in the third-round replay defeat at home to Orient on 16 January 1978?

9 Which Norwich player holds the club record for most FA Cup appearances during his time at the club?

10 Which club have Norwich played more often than any other club in the tournament*?

11 Which 1980s FA Cup Final saw two future Norwich managers on opposing sides?

*Up to and including the 2014/15 season.

Round 20

Millennium Canaries

Remember when aircraft were rumoured to be about to drop from the sky and all the world's computers were threatening to send themselves back to the Dark Ages? Ah yes, the millennium. It all seems so quaint and far away now. Yet it was meant to be the dawn of the Apocalypse. Which it clearly wasn't. Because that happened back in 1980 when we sold Kevin Reeves to Manchester City – or at least I thought it had. The following eleven questions all relate to the year 2000 and anything and everything in it that related to Planet Canary.

1   Who was Norwich City's manager on New Year's Day 2000?

2   Which player was the club's first signing of the millennium?

3   Remember our Swiss striker by the name of Giallanza? He made his Norwich debut from the bench in a 1–0 win over Wolves on 15 April 2000. What was his first name?

4 Why was the afternoon of Sunday, 19 March 2000 a particularly satisfying one for Bryan Hamilton?

5 When the Canaries travelled to Crewe on 4 March 2000, a member of the Crewe team who went on to win the game 1–0 would later have a short spell at Carrow Road with Norwich, name him?

6 Norwich didn't win a league game at Carrow Road in the 2000/01 season until a 4–2 win over Sheffield United on 21 October. Who was the former Hammer who scored the Canaries' 3rd goal in that game?

7 A former Footballer of the Year with 18 senior caps for England, he made 6 appearances for the Canaries in November 2000, can you name him?

8 Norwich won their second-round League Cup tie in the autumn of 2000 an impressive 8–3 on aggregate. Who were our opponents?

9   Who was manager of the Preston North End side that beat Norwich 1–0 on 17 October 2000 with a last-kick-of-the-game winner from Bjarni Gunnlaugsson?

10 Burdened with the label 'utility player' but good enough to be the only Norwich City player to start all 47 of the Canaries' league games throughout 2000, name him?

11 Which club did Norwich sign Alex Notman from for £250,000 in November 2000?

To Which Club?

More of the simple, straightforward stuff. Steak and kidney pie if you will, rather than all the highfalutin ones you get at some grounds. This is a companion to Round 8, the difference being that you have to name the clubs that these one-time Norwich City players joined (permanent rather than loan deals) when they left Carrow Road for the last time.

1 Iwan Roberts.

2 Jeremy Goss.

3 Simon Whaley.

4 Johnny Gavin.

5 Ian Culverhouse.

6 John Deehan.

7 Colin Suggett.

8 Lee Marshall.

9   Mick McGuire.

10 Marc Tierney.

11 Neil Adams.

Canary Mastermind

Settle down in the big black chair and take a deep breath. The following eleven questions are a selection of those that were used in BBC Radio Norfolk's 'Canary Mastermind' feature. Nobody ever got every single one of them right – can you break the mould here?

1 What was unique about Norwich's 2–0 League Cup victory over Luton Town at Kenilworth Road on 29 October 1985?

2 Who wore the number 9 shirt for Norwich when we played our first-ever game in top-flight football against Everton on 12 August 1972?

3 Why was the second leg of Norwich's 1973 League Cup semi-final against Chelsea at Carrow Road abandoned with only 5 minutes to play?

4 Name the Brazilian international who made his Newcastle debut against Norwich in September 1987?

5 Which Norwich City manager gave Craig Bellamy his Canaries debut?

6 What was the crowd chant that inevitably started up amongst Norwich fans whenever Percy Varco was playing for the Canaries?

7 Which former Norwich player has since managed Stirling Albion and Montrose, winning a promotion with Stirling in 1997?

8 Norwich used 36(!) different players during the 2006/07 season. Of those, twelve made fewer than 5 league appearances. How many of them can you name?

9 Three Norwich City players made their Canary debuts in the 3–3 draw at Wolves on 3 February 2009, amongst them the first Australian and the first New Zealander to play for the club. Name the players in question.

10 In Norwich's Championship-winning campaign of
    2003/04, who scored the Canaries' first league goal
    that campaign?

11 Name the one-time Norwich City player who scored
    goals in the 1999/2000 UEFA Cup and 2000/01
    Champions League competitions?

Round

23

The 1980s:
Part 2

The two-year contract for televised football signed between the football league and both the BBC and ITV in 1983 was just £5.2 million whilst the British transfer record at the beginning of the decade was £1,180,000. Meanwhile, at Carrow Road the players turned up on a matchday in cars that were just like the ones our dads drove. How come such a simpler age really wasn't that long ago? Another plunge into the Canaries' life and times in the 1980s ...

1 Four Canary league debuts came in the opening game of the 1985/86 season against Oldham – Mike Phelan, Kevin Drinkell, Garry Brooke and David Williams – which clubs did Norwich sign those players from?

2 Name the one-time Kings Lynn striker who made his debut for Norwich against Sunderland on 26 October 1985?

3 Norwich won the Division Two Championship in the 1985/86 season, finishing how many points ahead of runners-up Charlton?

4 Who opened the new Main Stand at Carrow Road in the 1–1 draw against Manchester City on 2 April 1987?

5 Which former Norwich player was appointed manager of Manchester City in 1987?

6 Name the former Norwich player who offered his services as manager 'initially for free' following the sacking of Ken Brown in November 1987?

7 Signed as a replacement for Steve Bruce, this unfortunate Canaries' career lasted just 34 minutes before injury on his debut forced him off and, eventually, brought about his retirement from the game. Can you name him and the club he made his debut against?

8 Four straight wins for the Canaries at the start of the 1988/89 season, which newly promoted side broke that run with a 2–2 draw at Carrow Road on 24 September?

9 Name the player who made his second debut for Norwich eight years after his first in the game at QPR on 2 January 1989.

10 Bryan Gunn was sent off during the 2–1 defeat at Coventry on 8 April 1989, which outfield Canary took his place in goal?

11 Name the Danish Under-21 forward who cost Norwich £360,000 from Aarhus in November 1989?

Round 24

The East Anglian Derby

You-know-who FC, our footballing Voldemort, the team that shall not be named. Voldemort was, of course, eventually overcome and vanquished, just as that lot down the A140 have been on numerous occasions. Here are eleven questions relating to our matches and relationship to our main East Anglian rivals, Diss Town. Oh go on then, Ipswich Town …

1   Name the six different competitions that Norwich and Ipswich have played each other in?

2   Who scored the Norwich goals in our 3–0 win over Ipswich on 20 March 1995 – the last time the two clubs played each other in the Premier League?

3   What was declared open prior to the 3–3 draw at Carrow Road on Boxing Day 1979?

4 Steve Bruce famously scored the decisive goal in the Canaries' 2–0 League Cup semi-final second-leg win over Ipswich at Carrow Road, sending Norwich to Wembley in the process, but who scored the first Norwich goal that evening?

5 Which former Ipswich player scored the opening goal in Norwich's 8–0 win over Sutton United in the 1989 FA Cup fourth round?

6 The club's first-ever meeting in the FA Cup was in 1962, Norwich winning a fourth-round replay 2–1 at Portman Road. In doing so, what did Norwich prevent Ipswich from doing that season?

7 Which former Norwich player was all set to sign for Ipswich in 1996 before seeing the yellow and green light and re-signing for the Canaries instead?

8 Name the odd one out: Peter Morris, Clive Woods, Keith Bertschin, Trevor Putney and Andy Marshall?

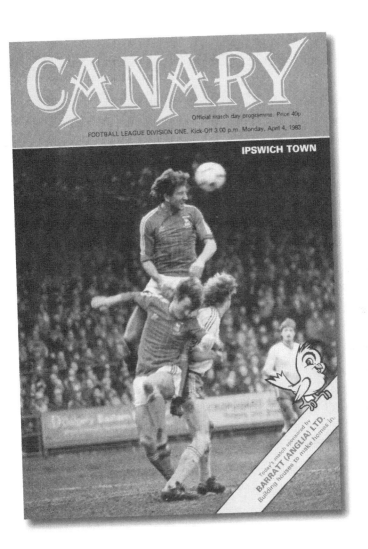

9 Referee Kevin Lynch awarded Ipswich two penalties in the game against Norwich on 19 November 1995. John Wark scored with the first, what happened with the second?

10 The 2010/11 season saw Norwich win the two Championship games between the sides 9–2 'on aggregate'. Who scored the last of Norwich's 9 goals in those two fixtures?

11 England's 5–1 win over Scotland at Wembley in 1975 saw Ipswich and Norwich players leading the line for England and Scotland respectively, who were they?

Round

25

Shirt Numbers

Have you got a player's name and number on the back of your shirt? In this round I'll name a famous Norwich City match and one of the players who scored in it – all you have to do is name the shirt number he was wearing on the day. Easy. Couzens-Lake 11.

1   Bayern Munich 1–2 Norwich City (1993).
    Jeremy Goss wore number?

2   Norwich City 3–2 Derby County (2011).
    Simeon Jackson wore number?

3   Norwich City 1–1 Everton (1972).
    Jimmy Bone wore number?

4   Norwich City 2–1 Newcastle United (2005).
    Youssef Safri wore number?

5   Norwich City 2–0 Manchester City (2001).
    Marc Libbra wore number?

6   Arsenal 2–4 Norwich City (1992).
    Mark Robins wore number?

7   Norwich City 4–4 Southampton (1989).
    Robert Rosario wore number?

8   Norwich City 1–0 Manchester United (2012).
    Anthony Pilkington wore number?

9   Manchester City 2–3 Norwich City (2013).
    Jonny Howson wore number?

10 Norwich 4–4 Middlesbrough (2005).
    Adam Drury wore number?

11 Norwich City 3–1 Manchester United (1959).
    Terry Bly wore number?

Obscure is the Word: Part 2

More Canary-related trivia that might be reasonably expected to fit into any other round yet no rounds at all. A smattering of questions that might require you to voyage to the event horizon of yellow and green. On the other hand, of course, you may well know the answers to them all.

I Which Norwich City manager steered the team to trophy success in the final of the Mr Clutch Cup?

2   Name the former Norwich great who boasted the admirable middle name of 'Stanford'?

3   With which football league club did former Canary striker Simeon Jackson launch his senior career?

4   Which Norwich player earnt the newspaper headline 'Daddy Cool' by scoring a vital winning goal for the Canaries in a Premier League game twenty-four hours after becoming a father for the first time?

5   Norwich used twenty-two different players during the 1992/93 campaign, the one which saw us finish third in the Premier League's debut season. Two of those players made only one league start, who were they?

6   The Canaries lost just one of their first nineteen league and League Cup games during the promotion-winning 1974/75 season. Name the team that got the better of us during the run.

7   Signed from Chester for £225,000 in July 1990, this Canary didn't make his debut for nearly a year after he was signed, can you name him?

8   Name the player who, after finishing a trial at Norwich in 1987, was immediately offered a place on the Canaries' schoolboy staff only to advise the club, 'I'm really sorry, but I have already signed at Manchester United.'

9   Norwich's league goals tally of 89 during the 2009/10 season was its best for fifty-one years. Those goals were shared around eighteen different scorers, how many of them can you name?

10 Norwich resumed life in the Championship in the 2014/15 season after three years in the Premier League. Who scored the club's first league goal that season?

11 Who was credited, albeit very tongue in cheek, with starting the move that led to Grant Holt's late winner in the 2–1 win over Reading in February 2011?

Round 27

The Swinging Sixties

The word is that if you can remember the 1960s then you weren't really there at all. Man. But what can you remember, recall or simply, for no apparent reason, just know about the Canaries and that rather colourful decade?

1   It's 1 January 1960. Happy New Year! Who was the manager of Norwich City on this date?

2   The Canaries' first game of the 1960s was a 2–0 win at Reading on 2 January, both goals coming from Terry Bly. He, rather surprisingly, left Norwich that summer for just £5,000, which club did he join?

3   Norwich won promotion to Division Two at the end of the 1959/60 season, their joint-leading goalscorer that season (with 16 league goals) repeating the feat the following campaign with another 16. Who was he?

4 League Cup glory for Norwich at the end of the 1961/62 season, beating Rochdale in the two-legged final. What was the aggregate score in that game, who was the Canaries' captain for that match and who was the manager?

5 Second Division Norwich knocked out two First Division clubs in their FA Cup campaign of the 1962/63 season, can you name them?

6 Another bit of 1960s FA Cup giant-killing. The Canaries knocked Manchester United out of the competition in the fourth round during the 1966/67 season with Gordon Bolland and Don Heath the scorers in our 2–1 win. Can you name the clubs that Bolland and Heath joined us from?

7 Bought from Luton Town for £35,000 in 1963, sold to Southampton (amidst much disquiet from the club's supporters) for £55,000 in 1966, can you name the player?

8　The Canaries fielded three different goalkeepers during their 1964/65 Division Two campaign, who were they?

9　Five different players captained Norwich during their 1968/69 Division Two campaign, how many can you name?

10　Norwich's opposition in their Division Two fixture against Stoke City on 9 March 1963 featured a player who was 48 years old, who was he?

11　It's New Year's Eve 1969 and the Seventies are coming! Who is the Norwich City manager on this date?

Round 28

The Lambert Years

Is it fair to say that the three years that Paul Lambert spent at the club as manager were amongst the most exciting in Norwich City's history? Quite possibly. This round focuses on all things Lambert and contains eleven questions relating to his time at the club. So put your shoulder to the wheel and give the lads a hand …

1   Who were the opposition in Lambert's first game as Norwich City manager?

2   The Canaries won only 2 of their first 7 league games of Lambert's tenure, name the teams we beat as part of that slow start?

3   With 44 league appearances from 46 games, this player made the most appearances for the Canaries in that League One title-winning season under Lambert, can you name him?

4 Norwich lost their opening game of the 2010/11 season 2–3 at home to Watford, a match that saw six Canaries make their first team debuts, who were they?

5 Name the centre-back signed on loan from Blackpool by Lambert in February 2011?

6 Norwich sealed promotion back to the Premier League with a 1–0 win at Portsmouth. One of the players in the Pompey line-up that night made his Canary debut in the opening game of the following season, a 1–1 draw at Wigan, who was he?

7 Name the player Norwich signed from Liverpool for £800,000 in the summer of 2011?

8 The Canaries rattled in 4 goals against Newcastle in an impressive 4–2 win over the Magpies at Carrow Road on 10 December 2011. Grant Holt scored 2 of the goals and Wes Hoolahan 1, who got the other Norwich goal?

9   Norwich were awarded just one penalty in the Premier
    League for the whole of the 2011/12 season – which
    team was it against, who was the scorer and what was
    the final score in that game?

10 Paul Lambert's last competitive win as Norwich City
    manager came against which team?

11 Where did Norwich finish in the table at the end of the
    2011/12 season?

Name the Ground

It's all about the away days. In this round you'll see eleven questions that contain information about a certain Norwich match, what you need to do with that information is work out who the opposition were and, from that, the ground we were playing on for that game. For example, 'Goss and Bowen stun illustrious hosts with first-half strikes' would be our 2–0 win over Bayern Munich in the 1993/94 UEFA Cup – so the answer is the Olympic Stadium, Munich. Easy ... off you go then.

1 Dave Stringer's first-half header seals a Championship triumph.

2 Paddon's hat-trick ensures League Cup shock.

3 A crowd of 67,633 see Allcock beat Hollowbread for surprise Canary FA Cup opener.

4 Ex-Man United striker goes on at half-time in debut and scores 2 in City comeback.

5   TV pundit's second-half own goal is opener in 2–0 Canary win, player cum future Norwich manager makes the points safe.

6   Fox's cross in the box leads to promotion joy.

7   David Corner lets Dixie in, the winning goal follows.

8   Namesake of Burnham Thorpe hero heads home to see us up.

9   New Norwich manager sees Robbo put his old team to the sword with a first-half double.

10 Peter Mendham gets the ball rolling as we become the first team to beat our hosts on their artificial surface.

11 A late Christmas present for all Canary fans as Drinkell secures our first-ever league win here in sixteen visits.

They Think
It's All Over ...

And indeed it is. Until the sequel. Well, you never know. However, as this is the end of the book as we know it, the eleven questions here will all focus on things that happened at the last minute, in the last minute or were the last of something or other, that sort of thing. A footballing final curtain in other words.

1 Who were the last team the Canaries played in a league game at The Nest?

2 The Canaries famously signed four players from Leeds United between July 2011 and January 2013, much to the accumulated ire of Leeds fans. Shame. Who was the last of that quartet to sign for the Canaries?

3 Who was John Bond's last signing for Norwich City as Canaries' boss?

4 Who scored the final Norwich goal in our 7–0 FA Cup win over Paulton Rovers in 2009?

5 Who scored the final Norwich goal in our 6–0 Championship win over Scunthorpe in 2011?

6 The Canaries were all set to name someone else as manager after John Bond left to join Manchester City in 1980. However, they quickly appointed Ken Brown when it was realised he wouldn't, as expected, be joining Bond at Maine Road. Can you name the man who missed out on being appointed Canaries' manager at the last moment?

7 Who scored the last-minute equaliser for the Canaries in the 1–1 at Everton in November 2012?

8 Who were the Canaries' opponents in the final game of Mike Walker's first spell in charge at Carrow Road?

9 Who was the final winner of the Barry Butler Memorial Trophy Player of the Season award of the twentieth century (i.e. the winner in 1999)?

10 Who scored the club's last goal in the 'old' First Division (i.e. our last league game at that level before the Premier League was introduced for the 1992/93 season)?

11 Who were our opponents in Kevin Keelan's final competitive game for the Canaries?

In the Beginning

1 1902.

2 The Criterion Cafe.

3 Either the Savoy Taylors Guild or Moss Bros. It's on White Lion Street. A plaque on the wall acknowledges its footballing significance.

4 Newmarket Road. The initial rent paid by the club for the site was £25 per annum.

5 The Norfolk & Suffolk League. The league existed right through to the 1963–64 campaign, after which it merged with the East Anglian League to form the Anglian Combination.

6 A friendly with Harwich & Parkstone which ended in a 1–1 draw.

7 Light blue and white halved shirts – the right-hand half was blue and the left half was white.

8 'In the days to call, which we have left behind.'

9 The 'Citizens' or 'Cits' for short. See answer to Q.10 below.

10 John Bowman, Middlesbrough-born and formally a QPR player. He is reported to have been the first person to make the connection between the football club and canaries, saying, upon his appointment '… I knew of the Cities existence, for in my schooldays, Geography was a favourite subject of mine, and I have since heard of the canaries'.*

11 Tottenham Hotspur. Norwich won 3–2 at The Nest on 30 January 1915.

*The Cities connection with canaries comes from European refugees, known collectively as the 'Strangers', who came to live in Norwich in the sixteenth century. Norwich was the centre of a large and successful textile industry that, by the 1600s, was struggling. More workers were needed and those that came over were from a region now covered by modern-day Belgium, France and the Netherlands were skilled in the trade. They were also famous for breeding canaries and thus, in time, the football club – the Canaries – became one of the Strangers' most famous legacies.

Into the Big Time!

1 Kevin Keelan, Clive Payne and Dave Stringer.

2 Ken Foggo.

3 Bristol City. Yes, a surprising one that – I'm assuming the large number of people who attended were swayed by the fact that it was played on the Tuesday evening after a long Easter weekend suffering countless visits by relatives.

4 David Cross, signed from Rochdale by Saunders for £40,000. Cross scored 30 goals in 131 league and cup games for the Canaries.

5 Partick Thistle. Bone scored for them in their shock 4–1 win over Celtic in the 1971 Scottish League Cup Final.

6 Geoffrey Watling, who was chairman at the time – he had prefaced the statement by saying, 'We weren't prepared to take no for an answer' – a most refreshing statement for any Canary fan to hear come from the man at the top.

7 Birmingham City.

8 Chelsea. They got to the final only to lose 2–1 to Stoke City.

9 Ron Wigg.

10 Birmingham City. The league game at Carrow Road ended 2–2.

11 Trevor Howard. He made 45 appearances from the bench in total for the Canaries, as well as being an unused number 12 on a further 20 occasions.

Canaries Before and After

1   Chris Woods for Nottingham Forest against Liverpool.
2   David Fairclough in his Liverpool days. Fairclough made just 2 Norwich appearances in 1985.
3   Ron Davies for Southampton, who signed him from Norwich in 1966. Following that game, Sir Matt Busby described Davies as the 'greatest centre forward in Europe'.
4   Martin Peters of Tottenham.
5   Andy Linighan for Arsenal in the FA Cup Final replay against Sheffield Wednesday in 1993.
6   Jim Whitley. And it's well worth seeing.
7   Willie Donachie, then at Manchester City.
8   David Hodgson for Liverpool against Roma. Hodgson played just 9 appearances for Norwich but scored 4 goals in that time.
9   Dave Watson for Everton against Manchester United.
10 Ted MacDougall in Bournemouth's 11–0 win over Margate in November 1971.
11 Willie Young.

Consolation Goals

1 Cody McDonald.
2 Greig Shepherd.
3 Rob Newman.
4 Darren Huckerby. It was his last goal as well as his final appearance in a Norwich City shirt.
5 Justin Fashanu.
6 Johnny Gavin.
7 Ken Foggo. The Canaries played 7 games in just nineteen days that April.
8 Steve Morison.
9 Iwan Roberts.
10 Robert Fleck.
11 Kevin Reeves.

Loan Canaries

1 Bobby Bell.
2 Ben Alnwick. His replacement, Fraser Forster, was also a loanee, coming in from Newcastle United.
3 Jan Molby.
4 Ryan Bertrand, Dean Carney, Alan Gow, Jonathan Grounds, John Kennedy, Chris Killen, Omar Koroma, Alan Lee, Adrian Leijer, Leroy Lita, Arturo Lupoli, David Mooney, Elliott Omozusi, Jason Shackell and Antoine Sibierski. Shackell, a former Norwich City player, joined on loan from Wolves, who bought him from Norwich in September 2008.
5 Kevin Harper, who joined from Portsmouth – yes, they really were in the Premier League then!
6 Peter Osgood.
7 Mike Pickering.
8 Harry Redknapp – 'arry made no competitive appearances for Norwich during his loan spell here.
9 Ryan Bertrand, who won the medal for Chelsea in 2012.
10 Louis Thompson.
11 Scott Parker.

The League Cup

1 Willie Reid. He resigned as Norwich City's manager a little over a week after that game.
2 Spotland, home of Rochdale United, the Canaries' opponents in that final.
3 Hugh Curran.
4 Gordon Chisholm, who diverted Asa Hartford's shot into the Sunderland goal.
5 David Hodgson. Some people may have answered with either Shaun Elliott, suspended for that game and therefore not eligible for selection, or Gary Rowell, who'd joined Norwich from Sunderland the previous summer.
6 Oldham Athletic.
7 Mel Machin.
8 Wolves, who went on to beat Manchester City 2–1 in the final.
9 Martin Peters and Martin Chivers.
10 2006. Ryan scored 2 goals in that game.
11 Gary Hooper (2) and Josh Murphy.

Who Was the First?

1 Mark Robins (69 minutes) in the 4–2 win over Arsenal on the opening day of the first Premier League season on 15 August 1992. The first Norwich player to score in the first half of a Premier League game was Lee Power who scored in the 15th minute of the 2–1 game at Crystal Palace on 29 August – Norwich's 5th league game that campaign!

2 Dave Watson in the 1985 League Cup win over Sunderland.

3 John Deehan, who signed Jon Newsome from Leeds for £1 million in 1994.

4 Phil Boyer* – his England debut was against Wales in 1976.

5 Gordon Bolland – he came on for Tommy Bryceland in the 3–0 defeat at home to Wolves on 2 October 1965.

6 Ted MacDougall *v.* Aston Villa in the 5–3 win at Carrow Road on 23 August 1975. Just to prove it wasn't a fluke, he did it again in the 4–2 home win against Everton a fortnight later.

7 Declan Rudd, who played there for England Under-16s in 2006.

8 Gary Megson against Ipswich Town on 18 December 1993.

9 John Bowman. John was also the club's first-ever manager, one of, at the time of writing, fourteen[†] men who have both played for, and managed, Norwich City.

10 Lee Power *v.* Ipswich Town on 18 December 1993. (See question 8 – clearly a bad day all round!)

11 Efan Ekoku in the 3–0 win over Vitesse Arnhem in September 1993.

*Anyone who knows me will expect me to say that it should have been Graham Paddon so here it is for you now. Because it should have been.

†John Bowman, James McEwen, Frank Buckley, Cecil Potter, Duggie Lochhead, Norman Low, Ron Ashman, Dave Stringer, John Deehan, Gary Megson, Martin O'Neill, Peter Grant, Bryan Gunn and Neil Adams.

From Which Club?

1 Watford (1989).
2 West Ham (1973).
3 Coventry City (1989).
4 Luton Town (1976).
5 QPR (1981).
6 Bristol City (1980).
7 Gillingham (1984).
8 Falkirk (2014).
9 Bristol Rovers (1982).
10 Brighton (2011).
11 Burnley (1985).

The 1970s: Part 1

Round 9

1 Ron Saunders. He took over on 1 July 1969. Three weeks later, man first walked on the moon.

2 Kenny Foggo with 17 goals. Scoring 15 in the league and 1 each in the FA and League cups. Peter Silvester was hard on his heels with 15, all scored in the league.

3 Kevin Keelan, Dave Stringer and, respect if you got this one, Clive Payne.

4 Jimmy Bone.

5 Millwall. They were in a promotion place (i.e. in at least second place) from mid-October 1971 to their last league game of the season, a 2–0 win over Preston on 29 April 1972. Three days later, Birmingham, who hadn't been in the top two all season, won 1–0 at Orient in their last game of the season to move into a top two position for the first time in that entire league campaign. Promotion came with it, at Millwall's expense. Gutted? I bet they were!

6 Paul Cheesley.

7 Ipswich Town. How good is that? It was 2–1 at Portman Road on 15 August 1972. Terry Anderson and Kenny Foggo scored the goals.

8 Graham Paddon. Who should have been the first Canary to play for England.

9 The Texaco Cup.

10 Everton. The Norwich fans protested at the manner of
the defeat by lobbing their blue (?) seat cushions on to the
pitch in protest.

11 Wolves, who went on to beat Manchester City, managed
by Ron Saunders, 2–1 in the final.

1 Poll & Withey Windows.
2 The Milk Cup.
3 Umbro. Yes, their little diamond-shaped logo appeared opposite the club badge at top left on that season's shirt.
4 Asics. I bought a pair of their trainers in support of the deal but couldn't wear them as it was like walking around with a couple of barges attached to my feet.
5 Yellow shorts. The kit itself was designed by Bruce Oldfield.
6 Ford.
7 Dunlop Tyres.
8 Screen Sports Supercup.
9 Xara.
10 Alexandra plc. This was an unusual arrangement to say the least as Alexandra were, and remain, more well known for manufacturing traditional workwear rather than sports kit, particularly football shirts.
11 Flybe (Flybe.com), the low-cost English airline based in Exeter.

Norwich are on the Telly Again

Round 11

1 Andy Townsend, now an ITV pundit himself, who seems to have forgotten that he ever played for us ('Well Clive, in my playing days at Southampton, Chelsea, Aston Villa, Middlesbrough and West Brom …').

2 Mark Robins, scoring against his former club. A sad night – had we won, we would have gone back to the top of the Premier League table, 5 points ahead of the Red Devils with 5 games to play. Who knows what might have happened?

3 John Devine, who we signed from Arsenal in 1983.

4 Rob Newman. His lofted ball into the Bayern Munich penalty area was headed out by Lothar Matthaus right into Gossy's stride.

5 Ian Crook, Lee Power and David Phillips (the latter with, according to Sky commentator Ian Darke, a 'right-foot rasper').

6 The win guaranteed our place in that season's play-offs by virtue of a sixth-place finish.

7 Wes Hoolahan.

8 Ian St John. Along with thousands of other Norwich City fans, I have never, nor will I ever, forgive him for nominating a Millwall player as his man of the match in spite of Norwich's impressive win, Robert Fleck's imperious winner and an absolutely superb display of goalkeeping by the real Man of the Match, Bryan Gunn.

9 Robert Snodgrass.

10 Peter Drury ('It's Roberts … the big man, the Welshman, in Cardiff, for Delia and the boss' – it didn't get much better than that – for around 11 minutes anyway).

11 Tranmere Rovers. If ever a televised Norwich game was worth a boot through the TV screen it was that one. We went into it on a run of 5 wins from 6 games, including a win over Leeds United six days earlier, and were 2 down in 11 soggy minutes, all that and a red card for Fraser Forster.

Ever-present

1 Chris Woods (1981/82, 82/83, 83/84 and 85/86).

2 John Ryan, a rampaging goalscoring full-back long before Gareth Bale (1977/78).

3 Ron Ashman (1950/51, 51/52, 52/53, 55/56, 59/60, 60/61 and 61/62).

4 Dave Stringer, Norwich captain, youth team coach and first team manager (1969/70, 71/72 and 73/74).

5 Steve Walford (1981/82).

6 Barry Butler, his name adorns the club's Player of the Year trophy. And rightly so (1958/59, 59/60, 60/61 and 61/62).

7 Mike Phelan. The question is a little misleading as he was an ever-present in the 1985/86 season but actually captained the side for 36 league games out of the 38 in the 1988/89 season (1985/86).

8 Johnny Gavin, 122 league goals between 1948 and 1955, a record which is highly unlikely to be broken (1950/51).

9 David Phillips (1989/90, 90/91 and 92/93).

10 Hugh Curran, sold to Wolves for £60,000 shortly after Morgan had said 'We won't sell him at any price'. Curran scored 53 goals in 124 league and cup appearances for the Canaries (1967/68).

11 Greg Downs (1983/84).

Record Breakers

1 Coventry City. The two clubs like high-scoring games when they play each other – there have also been (Norwich score first) a 6–2, 5–3, 3–5 and a 4–5.

2 The score was 8–0 against Sutton United in the fourth round of the FA Cup in 1989. It was also the biggest fourth-round victory for any side in the competition since 1960 when Tottenham beat Crewe 13–2 in a replay.

3 In the 1956/57 season. Not a good time to be a Canary fan. It included a run of 25 league games without a win, a 7–1 defeat at Torquay United and a humiliating exit in the first round of the FA Cup to non-league Bedford Town. Despite all this, Norwich still managed to score 61 league goals that season – the same number as they did in the 1992/93 season that saw the Canaries finish third in the Premier League – albeit having played 4 games fewer.

4 Jon Newsome, who signed from Leeds United.

5 Mark Bowen, who made 35 appearances for Wales whilst he was at Norwich.

6 Ralph Hunt in the 1955/56 season.

7 Martin O'Neill who represented Northern Ireland in the 1982 World Cup Finals in Spain.

8 Our highest-ever finish was third in the Premier League in the 1992/93 season and our lowest was the bottom (22nd) of Division Three South in 1930/31, finishing bottom of that league again (24th) at the end of the 1956/57 season. The Canaries were quite fortunate

as regards the former, as in both the previous season (1929/30) and following one (1931/32) the clubs that finished in 22nd place either failed in their bid for re-election to the league (Merthyr Town in 1930) or were wound up by their board of directors (Thames in 1932).

9 Ken Brown is the longest-serving Norwich City manager, taking charge of the first team for a total of 367 matches between 1980 and 1987. He is followed by John Bond (340) and Nigel Worthington (280). Bond then Brown were at the club as managers for fourteen years between them, Bond's spell lasting from 1973 to 1980.

10 Ron Davies, of whom, when he was in the process of signing for the Canaries, club chairman Geoffrey Watling said, 'If you fail your medical, we'll sack the doctor.'

11 First Division – Jimmy Bone; Premier League – Mark Robins; UEFA Cup – Efan Ekoku; and twenty-first century, depending on when you believe it began – Craig Fleming (2000) or Adrian Forbes (2001).

The scorer of the club's first-ever goal in a competitive league fixture was Victor Whitham, who joined Norwich from Barnsley for £50 in August 1920, scoring the Norwich goal in that first-ever league game for the Canaries, a 1–1 draw against Plymouth Argyle on 20 August 1920.

Britain's
Number One!

14

1 John Bond (throughout 1975).

2 Duncan Forbes (fit and back in the side as captain on 11 March 1972).

3 Graham Paddon *v.* Arsenal at Highbury in the League Cup quarter-final (21 November 1972).

4 Paul Lambert quits as Norwich City Manager (31 May 2012).

5 Justin Fashanu's goal of the season *v.* Liverpool, Barry Davies' commentary (9 February 1980).

6 Last game of Darren Huckerby's loan spell at Norwich City, the 4–1 win over Cardiff City at Carrow Road (13 December 2003).

7 Jeremy Goss' goal *v.* Leeds United at Elland Road in a 4–0 win (21 August 1993).

8 Fosters Lager (throughout 1987).

9 Michael Theoklitos debut match *v.* Colchester United and THAT 1–7 defeat at Carrow Road (8 August 2009).

10 Terry Bly's 2 goals in the 3–1 win over Manchester United in the FA Cup fourth round (10 January 1959).

11 Martin Peters who, with 12 league and cup goals, was the club's leading scorer at the end of the 1978/79 season (5 May 1979).

The 1980s:
Part I

1 Justin Fashanu (3), Dave Bennett and Greg Downs.
   Smartarse answer – Adrian Heath.
2 Dave Watson, Chris Woods and Steve Walford.
3 Luton Town (Champions) and Watford (runners-up).
   Newcastle United finished nineth whilst Chelsea finished
   in twelfth position in the Division Two table.
4 Ross Jack. Remember him? His 14 goals were made up of
   10 in the league plus 2 in the FA and League cups. When
   he signed for Norwich in 1979, Mel Machin was moved
   enough to refer to him as Norwich's own version of
   John Wark. Ross scored in 6 successive league games for
   the Canaries early in the 1981/82 season; a feat which,
   if equalled by a modern-day Norwich player, would
   probably make him worth £10 million overnight. As it was,
   we sold him to Lincoln City for £15,000 in 1983.
5 David Cross. The Manchester City side on that day featured
   six players who had either already played for Norwich or
   would go on to play for them later in their careers – Cross,
   of course, plus Joe Corrigan, Kevin Bond, Åge Hareide,
   Kevin Reeves and Asa Hartford.
6 Mark Barham.
7 Willie Young, sent home from training on one occasion by
   Mel Machin after he'd complained that 'we never ran in
   training at Arsenal'.
8 Dave Bennett, Mike Channon and Louie Donowa.

9 Paul Clayton. Paul was tipped to be one of THE stars from the victorious 1983 FA Youth Cup-winning side but only made 14 league appearances for Norwich.

10 Chris Woods and Joe Corrigan. If you were paying attention to the additional information on question 5, you'd have got this one.

11 Dennis Van Wijk. If you find yourself watching the highlights of the 1985 League Cup Final, watch the reaction from Chris Woods as the penalty is given – utter despair!

Great Scots

1 Asa Hartford. Asa was awarded the 'assist' for the goal that won the League Cup Final for Norwich in 1985, his shot going into Chris Turner of Sunderland's net via Gordon Chisholm.

2 Ted MacDougall. Ted was one of the considerable number of ex-Bournemouth players who joined their former manager, John Bond, when he swapped Dean Court for Carrow Road in 1973, although he came to Norwich through short spells and big fees via Manchester United and West Ham.

3 Robert Fleck, whose two spells at Norwich saw him score a total of 84 league goals, many of them truly memorable.

4 Bryan Gunn, who was sat on the Aberdeen bench along with Sir Alex Ferguson and all the other Aberdeen substitutes as they beat Real Madrid 2–1 in the 1983 Final of that competition.

5 Matt Crowe, who made a total of 56 league and cup appearances for the Canaries in that incredible 1958/59 season.

6 Paul Lambert. He was putting his shoulder to the wheel alongside his Motherwell teammates from 1993 to 1996.

7 Peter Grant, who won two Scottish Premier League titles and four Scottish cups with Celtic.

8 Ken Foggo. 'Kenny, Kenny Foggo, Kenny Foggo on the wing.'

9 Duncan Forbes. A player for whom the term 'Norwich Legend' sits very nicely indeed.

10 Gary Holt. I could have mentioned that he was a 'former army chef' but that would have made it too easy.

11 Bill Punton, who is now a matchday host at Carrow Road.

The 1970s:
Part 2

1 Peter Morris.
2 Manchester United, the final score over the two legs being
   3–2 in Norwich's favour. Three of the four semi-finalists
   were the teams that were promoted from Division Two
   at the end of that season, Aston Villa joining Norwich
   and the Red Devils. Fourth Division Chester made up
   the quartet.
3 Bradford City.
4 Nottingham Forest.
5 Viv Busby. Viv signed from Fulham for £50,000 (the same
   price, a ludicrously small one, that Norwich had sold
   MacDougall for) and ended that season as the Canaries'
   leading goalscorer with 11 goals from just 17 league games.
   This included a hat-trick against Leicester in Norwich's
   penultimate game of the season.
6 Peter Osgood. Sadly his impact was minimal,
   three low-key performances and no goals.
7 Middlesbrough.
8 No away win of any kind. Mind you, this was just the
   beginning as, during the 1978/79 season, the Canaries
   failed to win even one away game in the league. This was
   despite scoring 22 goals – more goals than nine of their
   divisional rivals, including Bristol City who only managed
   13 goals in their 21 league games away from home but
   managed to win 4 of them!

9 The Anglo-Scottish Cup – strangely named as the three fixtures that Norwich played in the competition were all against English clubs, and the Willhire Cup which saw wins over Cambridge United and Colchester United before losing to Ipswich Town in what was for them, after all, their cup final for that season.

10 Tampa Bay Rowdies.

11 John McDowell and Alan Taylor. Taylor scored the 2 goals that saw off Fulham in that match.

1 Ben Alnwick (from Tottenham); Fraser Forster (Newcastle
   United); Russell Martin (Peterborough United); Michael
   Rose (Stockport County); and Stephen Elliott (Preston
   North End). Martin joined us on loan in November 2009
   with the deal being made permanent the following February.

2 The Citizens or 'Cits' for short. The first-recorded reference
   to the club and the little yellow bird came about as the
   result of an interview given with newly appointed manager
   John Bowman in 1905 when, after he was asked what he
   knew about his new club, he said, '… I knew of the City's
   existence … I have heard of the canaries', the latter being
   a reference to the city's links in the fifteenth and sixteenth
   centuries to Flemish weavers who had brought the birds
   with them to Norfolk.

3 The Canaries were the last top-flight club not to be relegated
   after finishing the season in twentieth place (i.e. second from
   bottom). The three up/three down rule for promotion and
   relegation was first introduced for the 1974/75 season when,
   paradoxically, Norwich became the first club to be promoted
   after finishing in third place in the old Second Division. Luton
   Town, incidentally, became the first club to be relegated from
   the top flight after finishing in twentieth place that season.

4 Steve Bould for Arsenal, after 28 minutes.

5 Ruel Fox (2) and Chris Sutton. Mark Robins might have had
   the fourth had Gossy not barged him out of the way in order
   to connect and score the third with that magnificent volley.

6 Non-league Ilford, who were 1–0 up at half-time!
Bobby Brennan (2) and Jimmy Hill saw them off.

7 David Phillips.

8 Jim Duffy who was caretaker manager at the time, pending
the eventual appointment of Glenn Roeder.

9 Matt Gilks, the goalkeeper who we signed from Rochdale on
a free transfer in 2007. Gilks began the 2014/15 season as
cover for Tom Heaton at Premier League Burnley.

10 Barry Butler. Can you imagine a player signing for a
club and saying something like that now? It beats '…
the facilities here are great and the lads have made me feel
very welcome'. Butler was a one-off, gentleman and player.

11 Malcolm Allen with 7 goals in 5 games –
he didn't play in the third-round win over Port Vale.

The FA Cup

1 1959 (Luton Town), 1989 (Everton) and 1992 (Sunderland). Each of those teams went on to lose the final. Moral of the story? Don't knock Norwich out of the semi-final, nothing good will come of it.

2 Dave Watson. Dave had inherited the role from Martin O'Neill that season who, in turn, had taken over from Mick McGuire.

3 It took us that long to knock Birmingham City out at the third-round stage-four games, which ended 0–0 (away), 1–1 (home), 1–1 (away) and 1–0 (home). Games two and three went to extra time. A week later, finally, we knocked them out but then lost 2–1 to West Ham in the fourth round.

4 Luton are responsible for our joint record FA Cup defeat (6–0) in 1927, for knocking us out of the semi-finals in 1959 and for becoming the first non-league club to knock a top-flight side out of the FA Cup for nearly a quarter of a century in 2013 with their 1–0 win at Carrow Road.

5 We managed to exit at the third-round stage on every occasion.

6 Twice – losing to Nottingham Forest in 1991 and beating Southampton in 1992.

7 Ken Nethercott.

8 Jim Fleeting.

9 Ron Ashman, who made a total of 56 appearances in the FA Cup for us. To put that into some sort of perspective, if anyone was to play in 56 FA Cup games for the club now*, they would need to have played in our third-round replay defeat at Swindon Town on 13 January 1988, then, providing he played in all of our FA Cup games after that one, game 56 would have been our 3–0 exit at Fulham in another third-round replay, this one on 14 January 2014. That's just twenty-six years and 56 FA Cup matches for the Canaries – even if the player in question had made his Canary debut as a 17 year old, he would have been 43 by the time the Fulham game came around!

10 Brighton & Hove Albion, who we have met on 10 occasions in the FA Cup. Coventry City are next up with 9, followed by Sunderland with 7. Teams we have met just the once in the tournament include Bath City, Corinthians, Dorchester Town, Metrogas and Sheppey United.

11 The 1982 FA Cup Final saw future Norwich managers Chris Hughton (Tottenham) and Glenn Roeder (QPR) face each other at Wembley.

*Up to and including the 2013/14 competition.

1 Bruce Rioch.
2 You can have any of the four as they were all signed on the same day! Derrick 'Des' Hamilton, Garry Brady, Fernando Derveld and Raymond de Waard all arrived on loan at the club on 22 March 2000 – although Derveld had been offered a trial in February by Bruce Rioch, he'd decided not to offer the Dutchman terms. A month or so later, Bryan Hamilton thought differently and Derveld was offered a full-time playing contract.
3 Gaetano.
4 Hamilton's first game in charge of Norwich saw the Canaries travel to Portman Road to play his old team and win 2–0 thanks to 2 goals, 1 of which was a touch of genius from Iwan Roberts.
5 Full-back David Wright, who made 5 appearances on loan for Norwich in 2005. How many people thought it was Dean Ashton?
6 Tony Cottee. 8 games, 2 goals then off to Barnet as player manager.
7 Scott Parker.
8 Blackpool. A 3–3 draw at Carrow Road was followed by a remarkable 5–0 win at Bloomfield Road a fortnight later. City had five chances in the whole game and scored the lot.
9 David Moyes.

10 Daryl Sutch. 'Sutchy' is a somewhat understated and unappreciated part of the club's history. He did, however, play under eleven different managers during his time at the club, two of whom were caretakers, as well as making 352 senior appearances.

11 Manchester United. Notman's scoring record for the Red Devils included 21 goals in just 26 games for their 'B' side, which helped make him as much of a prospect as some of the more well-known youngsters to have come through from their youth side in the last couple of decades or so.

To Which Club?

1 Gillingham.
2 Charlton Athletic. Most people would answer with Hearts which is not the case. If you take time out to read Gossy's autobiography*, you'll learn about him leaving Norwich and signing for Charlton and Alan Curbishley only to realise, after a few days at the club, he'd made the wrong choice. Curbishley, to his credit, and Charlton agreed to release him from his contract and Gossy joined Hearts.
3 Chesterfield.
4 Watford.
5 Swindon Town. Cully made 97 league appearances for them.
6 Ipswich Town.
7 Newcastle United.
8 Leicester City.
9 Barnsley.
10 Bolton Wanderers.
11 Oldham Athletic. It was Neil's second spell with the club, he'd previously been with them from 1989 to 1994 and was one of John Deehan's early signings for Norwich when he moved here for £250,000 in February 1994.

*Gossy the Autobiography by Jeremy Goss and …
Edward Couzens-Lake (I have no shame).

Canary Mastermind

1 It was Luton's first defeat on their plastic pitch which was installed at the beginning of that season.

2 David Cross.

3 Fog – according to Keith Skipper in the EDP, 'The Canaries last night had to endure the sort of hideous torment Hammer Films reserve for their most sinister villains.'

4 Mirandinha – subject of one of the best football songs I have ever heard from an opposing crowd.
'His name is Mirandinha, he's not from Argentina, he's from Brazil, he's f***ing brill!'

5 Mike Walker in the game against Crystal Palace on 15 March 1997.

6 'Give it to Varco' – namely, Percy Varco. And no wonder, the man was dynamite with a football at his feet. He made a total of 65 league and cup appearances for Norwich scoring 47 goals – which included 10 in 8 appearances during the FA Cup.

7 Kevin Drinkell.

8 Jamie Ashdown, Patrick Boyle, Chris Brown, Lee Camp, Luke Chadwick, Robert Eagle, Craig Fleming, Ryan Jarvis, David Marshall, Kris Renton, Michael Spillane and Peter Thorne.

9 David Carney (Australia) and Chris Killen (New Zealand). The other was Alan Gow.

10 Mark Rivers. He started that season with some intent, scoring 4 goals in our first 3 games.

11 Darren Huckerby during his spell at Leeds United.

1 Burnley, Grimsby, Tottenham and Bristol Rovers. Young and hungry? Almost. David Williams was 30 when Ken Brown signed him and had already spent two of his ten years at Bristol Rovers as first team manager!

2 Wayne Biggins. 'Bertie' was signed from Burnley.

3 They were 7 points ahead.

4 The Duchess of Kent. She officially opened it for the game against Manchester City on 14 February, the game ending 1–1 with current Ipswich manager Mick McCarthy getting booked for his part in a spot of handbags with Robert Rosario.

5 Mel Machin. Mel tried to sign Jeremy Goss from Norwich whilst he was in charge of Manchester City and later on at Barnsley when he was manager at Oakwell.

6 Mike Channon, who later claimed it was a serious offer.

7 John O'Neill. The opposition were Wimbledon.

8 Millwall. Following that game, Norwich were first in Division One with Millwall third.

9 Alan Taylor. Most famous for scoring both of West Ham's goals in the 1975 FA Cup Final against Fulham, Taylor originally signed for Norwich from the Hammers in 1979. He re-signed for the Canaries after subsequent spells with Vancouver Whitecaps, Cambridge United, Hull City, Burnley and Bury, in August 1988; his one start and goal in his second spell coming in that game at Loftus Road.

10 Mark Bowen. No substitute goalies back then!

11 Henrik Mortensen.

The East
Anglian Derby*

1 The Football League/Premier League (counts as one), the FA Cup, League Cup, Texaco Cup, Zenith Data Systems Cup and the Simod Cup.

2 Jamie Cureton, Ashley Ward and Darren Eadie.

3 It was the first game played in front of the newly opened River End.

4 John Deehan.

5 Trevor Putney.

6 By knocking them out of the FA Cup, we prevented the all-too-horrendous possibility of their doing the League and FA Cup double as they managed, miraculously, to win the league title that season.

7 Ian Crook. All set to sign for Ipswich before Mike Walker helped him see the light and return to Norwich.

8 Andy Marshall. He went from Norwich to Ipswich; all of the other players went from Ipswich to Norwich.

9 He awarded Ipswich a second penalty before changing his mind, much to the consternation of both the Ipswich players and their few dozen supporters at the game.

10 Daniel Pacheco.

11 David Johnson (Ipswich) played centre forward for England, Ted MacDougall (Norwich) for Scotland. Johnson scored England's 5th goal whilst MacDougall won Scotland's penalty from which a future Norwich manager, Bruce Rioch, scored.

*'Don't call it the Old Farm Derby. It's the East Anglian Derby' – Rob Butler, BBC Radio Norfolk.

Shirt Numbers

1 11.

2 10. Doubly famous, of course, for not only the drama of the occasion but BBC Radio Norfolk's Chris Goreham and his utter ecstasy as the ball found its way into the Derby net.

3 8.

4 15.

5 19. And unforgettable.

6 12. Robins, who was sent on in the second half with Norwich 2–0 down and looking at, as one player later told me, 'damage limitation', was probably given the equivalent of the age-old refrain from Mike Walker as he took to the pitch, '… go on son, help us win it' – which he promptly did!

7 9. ITV's Goal of the Season.

8 12.

9 8.

10 3.

11 9.

1 Mike Bassett in the film *Mike Bassett: England Manager*. The Canaries beat Leicester City 3–2 in the final.

2 Martin Peters.

3 Rushden & Diamonds.

4 John Polston, who later confessed that his wife 'nearly fell off the bed' when he told her that he'd scored the winner at Carrow Road with Norwich defeating Aston Villa 1–0.

5 Efan Ekoku and Andy Johnson.

6 Fulham. It had to be really, didn't it? They turned us over 4–0 at Craven Cottage on 21 September 1974. It was Roger Hansbury's debut for the Canaries.

7 Colin Woodthorpe, who went on to make 161 league appearances for the Canaries.

8 David Beckham. He was then advised by Canary coach Kit Carson that if he was ever rejected by the Red Devils, there would be a place for him at Norwich City. Sadly for Norwich, that was never the case.

9 In alphabetical order – Jens Berthel Askou (2); Jamie Cureton (2); Gary Doherty (5); Stephen Elliott (2); Grant Holt (24); Wes Hoolahan (11); Stephen Hughes (3); Oli Johnson (4); Chris Martin (17); Cody McDonald (3); Anthony McNamee (1); Michael Nelson (3); Jon Otsemobor (1); Michael Rose (1); Darel Russell (3); Korey Smith (4); Michael Spillane (1) and Owain Tudur-Jones (1). Plus 1 own goal, courtesy of Brighton's Tony Elphick.

10 Bradley Johnson in the 3–0 win at Carrow Road
over Watford.

11 Chief Executive David McNally who 'started' the move by
throwing a loose ball that had ended up in the directors'
box back into play.

1 Archie Macaulay.
2 Peterborough United. The story goes that the Canary hierarchy felt that Bly's on-going problems with his knee meant he would no longer be effective as a player. He went on to score 52 goals in his first season with Peterborough.
3 Terry Allcock.
4 Aggregate score was 4–0. Ron Ashman was Norwich City captain and Willie Reid the manager.
5 Blackpool (3–1 in a replay after a 1–1 draw at Carrow Road) and Manchester City (2–1 at Maine Road).
6 Bolland joined the club from Orient whilst Heath made the long trip north from Middlesbrough.
7 Ron Davies. Geoffrey Watling had, when Davies signed, threatened to sack the club doctor if he didn't pass Davies as medically fit to play for Norwich at the time. Maybe he should have sacked whoever was behind Davies' sale to Southampton?
8 Sandy Kennon (fairly easy), Kevin Keelan (easy) and Geoff Barnard (tricky).
9 Alan Black, Freddie Sharp, Laurie Brown, Terry Anderson and Ken Mallender.
10 Stanley Matthews. Norwich spoilt his day by winning 6–0.
11 Ron Saunders.

The Lambert Years

1 Brentford. Lambert watched from the stands.
2 Wycombe Wanderers (5–2) and Hartlepool (0–2).
3 Simon Lappin, the one and only King of Spain.
4 John Ruddy, Elliott Ward, Andrew Surman, David Fox,
  Andrew Crofts and Simeon Jackson.
5 Rob Edwards.
6 Ritchie de Laet.
7 Daniel Ayala.
8 Steve Morison.
9 Blackburn Rovers, Grant Holt, 3–3. Holty scored in the 4th
  minute of injury time.
10 Aston Villa, the club he eventually joined.
11 Twelfth.

Name the Ground

1 Vicarage Road, Watford. Stringer's opener in the 1–1 draw back in April 1972 earnt Norwich the point they needed to win the Division Two title. It was the Canaries' 8th game in just twenty-nine days.

2 Highbury. Paddon's hat-trick came in the League Cup fifth round in November 1972, with Norwich beating Arsenal 3–0.

3 White Hart Lane, scene of our FA Cup fifth-round game against Tottenham in 1959. John Hollowbread, the Tottenham goalkeeper for that game, spent twelve years at the club but made only 67 league appearances.

4 Highbury. Mark Robins came on at half-time in this opening-day fixture of the Premier League in August 1992 and scored twice as Norwich came from 2–0 down to win 4–2 against Arsenal.

5 Anfield. It's 1983 and after Mark Lawrenson's own goal puts Norwich ahead against Liverpool, Martin O'Neill adds a second to give us a 2–0 win.

6 Fratton Park, 2011. David Fox's cross to the advancing Simeon Jackson was a work of footballing art, the resultant goal sealing our 1–0 win against Portsmouth and a return to the Premier League.

7 Wembley, the 1985 League Cup Final against Sunderland. Corner is only in the Sunderland side because of an injury to Shaun Elliott (who would later join Norwich), his dithering near the corner flag led to Dixie Deehan dispossessing him. The rest, as they say, is history.

8 The Valley, Michael Nelson's header against Charlton Athletic earning us a 1–0 win and the points that guaranteed a quick return to the Championship.

9 Portman Road. Bryan Hamilton had just taken over from Bruce Rioch in March 2000 and would have been watching with probable mixed feelings as 2 goals from Iwan Roberts earnt Norwich a surprise 2–0 win at Ipswich.

10 Kenilworth Road, home of Luton Town and their, at the time, artificial pitch. We were the first team to win there against them in a 1985 League Cup game.

11 Old Trafford. Our first-ever league victory at the home of Manchester United in 1986.

They Think It's All Over ...

I Swansea Town as they were then known. But Swansea City is acceptable. The game was played on 4 May 1935 and ended in a 2–2 draw, Billy Warnes and Ken Burditt scoring the goals. Burditt also scored in the first league game to be played at Carrow Road a little under four months later.

2 Luciano Becchio.

3 Dražen Mužinić. He was, at the time, our £350,000 record signing. Bond chose not to take him to Manchester City with him.

4 Chris Martin.

5 Simeon Jackson. A rare case of two players getting a hat-trick in the same match as Grant Holt had already done so for Norwich, Jacko's last-minute goal being the final one of his hat-trick.

6 John Benson. He'd been offered the post of caretaker manager after Bond's departure to Manchester City and was all set to take it with the proviso that it would be a full-time appointment, only for Arthur South to hurriedly appoint Ken Brown instead when it became clear Brown would not be accompanying Bond to Maine Road.

7 Sébastien Bassong.

8 The final match of Mike Walker's first spell in charge at Norwich was the 2–1 defeat to Newcastle United on 4 January 1994, Mark Bowen scoring the final goal of Walker's time at the helm.

9 Iwan Roberts won the award in 1999. He also won it in 2000 so the pedants who argue that the year 2000 was actually the final one of the twentieth century will also be right if they gave Roberts as their answer!

10 Our last-ever top-flight goal prior to the formation of the Premier League was scored by Robert Fleck in the 1–1 draw at home to Wimbledon on 25 April 1992. Fleck's replacement at Norwich, Mark Robins, duly scored our first-ever Premier League goal the following August against Arsenal.

11 Keelan's 673rd and final first team appearance for Norwich was in the game against Liverpool at Carrow Road on 9 February 1980.

Bibliography

Much of this book is my original work, gained and retained at matches and with myriad fans of the greatest team in the world. Football fans love trivia (hello NCFC fan and trivia master David 'Spud' Thornhill) and I'm no exception. However, there have been some invaluable sources for checking and rechecking of facts and statistics, so thanks and much respect to the following …

Davage, Mike, *Glorious Canaries Past & Present 1902–1994* (Norwich City FC, 1994).

Davage, Mike, Eastwood, John & Platt, Kevan, *Canary Citizens Centenary Edition* (Jarrold Publishing, 2001).

Eastwood, John & Davage, Mike, *Canary Citizens – The Official History of Norwich City FC* (Almedia Books, 1986).

Hadgraft, Rob, *Norwich City The Modern Era – A Complete Record* (Desert Island Books, 2003).

Hadgraft, Rob, *Norwich City The Modern Era – A Complete Record 1980–2010* (Desert Island Books, 2010).

About the Author

EDWARD COUZENS-LAKE threw off the corporate shackles in 2010 in order to become a full-time writer. *Never Mind the Canaries* is his sixth book about Norwich City Football Club, a literary commitment to the Canaries that also includes a regular feature in the club's matchday programme and his stint as question master and researcher for 'Canary Mastermind', a popular feature on BBC Radio Norfolk's McVeigh & Butler show Norfolk-born and proudly so, he currently lives near Chichester with his wife and numerous cats.

Also from The History Press

BACK OF THE NET!

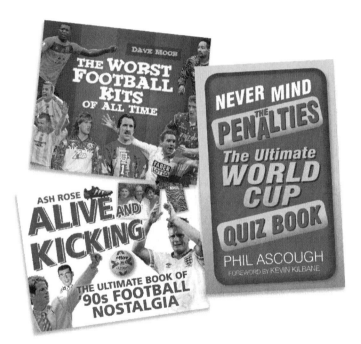

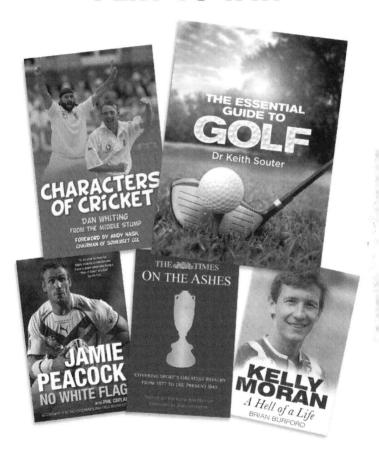

Printed in Great Britain
by Amazon